Prophetic Jewels

صلى الله عليه وسلم

A collection of
40 short Hadith
spoken by the
Best of Creation

by Ahmed Abdo

Prophetic Jewels

First published 2022

Published by QUL College

PO BOX 191 Revesby NSW 2212

Email: info@qulcollege.com

https://www.qulcollege.com

Prophetic Jewels

Abdo, Ahmed

ISBN: 978-0-64565-490-5 *paperback*
ISBN: 978-0-64565-491-2 *ebook*

Contents

Introduction

In the Name of Allāh, Most Gracious, Supremely Compassionate

All praise is due to *Allāh*, the One Who granted human beings the marvellous ability of expression, and peace and blessings be upon our Master *Muḥammad*, the most eloquent of creation.

In an age where speech is conveyed in the blink of an eye, it is ever more important to lend an attentive ear to the words uttered by the best of creation; the one whom *Allāh* loves more than any other creature. The speech of our Messenger *Muḥammad*, peace be upon him, is a delight for our tongues to repeat and our hearts to ponder upon.

Allāh reminds us in the *Qur'ān* to *'speak beautifully to people'* (2:83). If we were to search far and wide for the best speech of human beings, we would not find anyone more beautiful in form, character, words, actions, thoughts and intentions than the final Prophet and Messenger *Muḥammad*, peace be upon him.

One of the primary objectives of this collection is to encourage and motivate people all around the world to become more aquainted with the lofty wisdom and speech of the Prophet *Muḥammad*, peace and blessings of *Allāh* be upon him. The *ḥadīth* (sayings) selection contained in this book have been curated over a span of several years.

To get to know someone well, you need to observe their character and reflect upon their speech. This book provides the inquisitive reader a window to peer upon the thoughts, inclinations, and wisdom of the man whom Muslims revere as the last Prophet to be sent to humankind - spreading mercy from an All-Merciful Lord.

Despite our living in an age of rising scepticism, we continue to observe young Muslims becoming more and more attached to the life, speech and character of the Prophet *Muḥammad*, peace be upon him. *Allāh* Almighty describes the speech of the Prophet in the following words:

'And he does not speak from his own desire,
rather it is a revelation revealed.' *Qur'ān* 53:3-4

Using this book, we have taught children from the age of five to recite, memorise and understand the meanings of these Prophetic sayings. Students would properly pronounce the words contained in each *ḥadīth*, taking note of correct vowel marks in Arabic. I have made the English transliteration available to facilitate the reading for those unable to read the original Arabic script. The transliteration serves to display the Arabic words as pronounced in the oral form. I found this to be a more accurate and effective method, since the reader who will rely on the transliteration would be looking to pronounce the *ḥadīth* exactly as it is recited in the Arabic language.

In this published edition, I have made an effort to note the source of each *ḥadīth*. Although these sources did not appear in the original version we used for our young students, I felt it would be important for the reader to see from which collections of *ḥadīth* they have been selected. Many *ḥadīth* would be traced back to multiple collections, however for the sake of brevity, only the main collections have been noted for each *ḥadīth* in this book.

To assist you, your students and your children in perfecting the pronunciation of each *ḥadīth*, I invite you to visit:

https://qulcollege.com/hadith

Here you will find multimedia resources with high quality audio recordings for each *ḥadīth* in Arabic and English. I hope they are of benefit to you in your journey to adorning your tongue and heart with the words of our Beloved Messenger *Muḥammad*, peace be upon him.

Ahmed Abdo
1 Rabīʿ al-Thāni 1444 AH
27 October 2022 CE

Prophetic Jewels

صلى الله عليه وسلم

Hadīths 1-40

Instructions

You will notice four sections on each *ḥadīth* page:

1. Arabic script
2. English transliteration
3. English translation
4. Source of the *ḥadīth*

When reciting and memorising each *ḥadīth*, begin with:

قَالَ رَسُولُ اللهِ ﷺ

qāla rasūlullāhi
ṣallallāhu ʿalayhi
wa ālihi wa ṣaḥbihi
wa sallam

This means 'The Messenger of Allah, peace and blessings of Allah be upon him, his family, and his companions, said: ...'

The above words were included in the Arabic script on each page, but not in the transliteration and translation for sake of brevity.

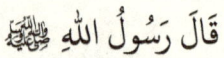

Hadith 1

قَالَ رَسُولُ اللهِ ﷺ

الْجَنَّةُ تَحْتَ أَقْدَامِ الأُمَّهَاتِ

al-jannatu taḥta
aqdāmil ummahāt

"Paradise lies at
the feet of Mothers."

al-Khaṭīb al-Baghdādi
in al-Jāmiʿ 1702

Hadith 2

قَالَ رَسُولُ اللهِ ﷺ

يَا غُلَامُ سَمِّ اللَّهَ
وَكُلْ بِيَمِينِكَ وَكُلْ مِمَّا يَلِيكَ

yā ghulām
sammillāh wa kul bi yamīnik
wa kul mimmā yalīk

"O child:
Mention the name of *Allāh*,
eat with your right hand,
and eat from what is
in front of you."

Ṣaḥīh Bukhāri 5376
Ṣaḥīh Muslim 2022

Hadith 3

قَالَ رَسُولُ اللهِ ﷺ

الْمَرْءُ مَعَ مَنْ أَحَبَّ

al-marʾu maʿa
man aḥab

"A person will
be with the
one whom
they love."

Ṣaḥīh Bukhāri 6168
Ṣaḥīh Muslim 2640

Hadith 4

قَالَ رَسُولُ اللهِ ﷺ

خَيْرُكُمْ مَنْ تَعَلَّمَ الْقُرْآنَ وَعَلَّمَهُ

khayrukum man
taʿallamal qurʾāna
wa ʿallamah

"The best among
you is the one who
learns and teaches
the *Qurʾān*."

Ṣaḥīh Bukhāri 5027

Hadith 5

قَالَ رَسُولُ اللهِ ﷺ

لَا آكُلُ وَأَنَا مُتَّكِئٌ

lā ākulu
wa anā muttakiʾ

"I do not eat
while leaning."

Ṣaḥīh Bukhāri 5399

Hadith 6

قَالَ رَسُولُ اللَّهِ ﷺ

زَيِّنُوا الْقُرْآنَ بِأَصْوَاتِكُمْ

zayyinul qurʾāna
bi aṣwātikum

"Beautify the *Qurʾān*
with your voices."

Sunan al-Nasāʾi 1015

Hadith 7

قَالَ رَسُولُ اللهِ ﷺ

بَرُّوا آبَاءَكُمْ تَبَرَّكُمْ أَبْنَاؤُكُمْ

barrū ābā'akum
tabarrakum abnā'ukum

"Be obedient to
your parents,
and your children
will be obedient
to you."

Mustadrak al-Ḥākim 7259

Hadith 8

قَالَ رَسُولُ اللهِ ﷺ

قُلْ هُوَ اللَّهُ أَحَدٌ

تَعْدِلُ ثُلُثَ الْقُرْآنِ

qul huwallāhu aḥad
taʿdilu thuluth al-qurʾān

"The Sūrah: '*Say: He is Allah, The One*', is equivalent to a third of the *Qurʾān*."

Ṣaḥīh Muslim 811

Hadith 9

قَالَ رَسُولُ اللهِ ﷺ

خِيَارُكُمْ أَحَاسِنُكُمْ أَخْلاَقًا

khiyārukum
aḥāsinukum akhlāqā

"The best among
you are the best
in character."

Sunan al-Tirmidhi 1975

Hadith 10

قَالَ رَسُولُ اللهِ ﷺ

بَيْنَ كُلِّ أَذَانَيْنِ صَلاَةٌ لِمَنْ شَاءَ

bayna kulli adhānayn
ṣalātun li man shā’

"There is a prayer
between the two
calls (*adhāns*) for
the one who
wants to pray."

Ṣaḥīh Bukhāri 627

Hadith 11

قَالَ رَسُولُ اللهِ ﷺ

مَنْ صَامَ رَمَضَانَ إِيمَانًا وَاحْتِسَابًا
غُفِرَ لَهُ مَا تَقَدَّمَ مِنْ ذَنْبِهِ

man ṣāma ramaḍāna
īmānan waḥtisāban
ghufira lahu mā taqaddama
min dhanbih

"A person who fasts the month
of *Ramaḍān*, having faith in *Allāh*
and seeking reward from Him,
all their past sins will be forgiven."

Ṣaḥīh Bukhāri 2014
Ṣaḥīh Muslim 760

Hadith 12

قَالَ رَسُولُ اللهِ ﷺ

أَحَبُّ الْبِلَادِ إِلَى اللهِ مَسَاجِدُهَا
وَأَبْغَضُ الْبِلَادِ إِلَى اللهِ أَسْوَاقُهَا

aḥabbul bilādi ilallāhi masājiduhā
wa abghaḍul bilādi ilallāhi aswāquhā

"The most beloved of places
to *Allāh* are the mosques,
and the most hated of places
to *Allāh* are the marketplaces."

Ṣaḥīh Muslim 671

Hadith 13

قَالَ رَسُولُ اللهِ ﷺ

الْبَخِيلُ مَنْ ذُكِرْتُ عِنْدَهُ فَلَمْ يُصَلِّ عَلَيَّ

al-bakhīlu man dhukirtu
ʿindahu falam yuṣalli ʿalayy

"The miserly person is the one who upon my mention, does not send prayers upon me."

Musnad Aḥmad 1736

Hadith 14

قَالَ رَسُولُ اللهِ ﷺ

الْخَلْقُ كُلُّهُمْ عِيَالُ اللهِ
فَأَحَبُّهُمْ إِلَى اللهِ أَنْفَعُهُمْ لِعِيَالِهِ

al-khalqu kulluhum ʿiyālullāh
fa aḥabbuhum ilallāhi
anfaʿuhum li ʿiyālih

"All creation are dependent upon *Allāh*. The most beloved of creatures to *Allāh* are those who are most beneficial to His dependents."

Musnad Abu Yaʿlā 3370

Hadith 15

قَالَ رَسُولُ اللهِ ﷺ

جَدِّدُوا إِيمَانَكُمْ

قِيلَ: يَا رَسُولَ اللهِ وَكَيْفَ نُجَدِّدُ إِيمَانَنَا؟

قَالَ: أَكْثِرُوا مِنْ قَوْلِ لَا إِلَهَ إِلا اللهِ

jaddidū īmānakum
qīla yā rasūlallāh
wa kayfa nujaddidu īmānanā
qāla akthirū min qawli
lā ilāha illallāh

"'Renew your faith.'
The Companions asked:
'O Messenger of *Allāh*,
how can we renew our faith?'
He said: 'Be abundant in your saying
there is no God but *Allāh*.'"

Musnad Aḥmad 8710

Hadith 16

قَالَ رَسُولُ اللهِ ﷺ

حُفَّتِ الْجَنَّةُ بِالْمَكَارِهِ
وَحُفَّتِ النَّارُ بِالشَّهَوَاتِ

ḥuffatil jannatu bil-makārih
wa ḥuffatin-nāru bish-shahawāt

"Paradise is surrounded
by hardships, and
Hellfire is surrounded
by temptations."

Ṣaḥīh Muslim 2822

Hadith 17

قَالَ رَسُولُ اللهِ ﷺ

رَكْعَتَانِ بِسِوَاكٍ خَيْرٌ
مِنْ سَبْعِينَ رَكْعَةٍ بِدُونِ سِوَاكٍ

rakʿatāni bi siwākin khayrun min
sabʿīna rakʿatin bidūni siwāk

"Two units of prayer
performed with
a *siwāk* are better
than seventy units
of prayer performed
wihout a *siwāk*."

Translator's note: A siwāk is a traditional tooth and mouth cleaning twig or root. It is taken from the Salvadora Persica (arāk) tree.

al-Afrād lil-Dāraquṭni

Hadith 18

قَالَ رَسُولُ اللهِ ﷺ

عَلَيْكُمْ بِالصِّدْقِ
فَإِنَّ الصِّدْقَ يَهْدِي إِلَى الْبِرِّ
وَإِنَّ الْبِرَّ يَهْدِي إِلَى الْجَنَّةِ

ʿalaykum biṣ-ṣidqi
fa innaṣ-ṣidqa yahdī ilal-birri
wa innal birra yahdī ilal-jannah

"Adhere to truth,
for truth leads
to good deeds
and good deeds
lead to Paradise."

Ṣaḥīh Muslim 2607

Hadith 19

قَالَ رَسُولُ اللهِ ﷺ

طَلَبُ الْحَلَالِ وَاجِبٌ
عَلَى كُلِّ مُسْلِمٍ

ṭalabul ḥalāli wājibun
ʿalā kulli muslim

"Seeking the lawful
is obligatory upon
every Muslim."

Musnad al-Firdaws lil-Daylami

Hadith 20

قَالَ رَسُولُ اللهِ ﷺ

غَنِيمَةُ مَجَالِسِ الذِّكْرِ الْجَنَّةُ

ghanīmatu
majālisi-dh-dhikr
al-jannah

"The reward for
attending gatherings
of the remembrance
of *Allāh* is Paradise."

Musnad Aḥmad 6651

Hadith 21

قَالَ رَسُولُ اللهِ ﷺ

كَلِمَتَانِ خَفِيفَتَانِ عَلَى اللِّسَانِ
ثَقِيلَتَانِ فِي الْمِيزَانِ حَبِيبَتَانِ إِلَى الرَّحْمَنِ
سُبْحَانَ اللهِ وَبِحَمْدِهِ سُبْحَانَ اللهِ الْعَظِيمِ

kalimatāni khafīfatāni 'alal-lisāni
thaqīlatāni fil-mīzāni
ḥabībatāni ilar-raḥmāni
subḥānallāhi wa bi ḥamdihi
subḥānallāhi-l-'adhīm

"Two expressions that are light
on the tongue, heavy in the scale,
and beloved to The All Merciful.
'*Glory be to Allah, and His is the Praise.*
He is free from any imperfection,
the Magnificent.'"

Ṣaḥīh Bukhāri 6682

Ṣaḥīh Muslim 2694

Hadith 22

قَالَ رَسُولُ اللهِ ﷺ

الرَّجُلُ عَلَى دِينِ خَلِيلِهِ
فَلْيَنْظُرْ أَحَدُكُمْ مَنْ يُخَالِلُ

ar-rajulu ʿalā dīni khalīlihi
fal-yandhur aḥadukum
man yukhālil

"A person follows the religion
of their friend, so you should
think about whom you
make your friend."

Sunan al-Tirmidhi 2378

Hadith 23

قَالَ رَسُولُ اللهِ ﷺ

إِذَا أَحَبَّ الرَّجُلُ أَخَاهُ
فَلْيُخْبِرْهُ أَنَّهُ يُحِبُّهُ

idhā aḥabbar-rajulu akhāhu
fal-yukhbirhu annahu yuḥibbuh

"When a man
loves his brother,
he should tell him
that he loves him."

Translator's note: Although the Arabic form of the hadith mentions the masculine form, it is equally applicable in the feminine form. Thus, a female may also inform her sister that she loves her. In both cases, this refers to a love for the sake of Allāh.

Sunan Abu Dāwūd 5124

Hadith 24

قَالَ رَسُولُ اللهِ ﷺ

بَشِّرُوا وَلاَ تُنَفِّرُوا
وَيَسِّرُوا وَلاَ تُعَسِّرُوا

bash-shirū walā tunaffirū
wa yassirū walā tuʿassirū

"Give glad tidings and
do not turn people away,
make things easy and
do not make matters
hard upon them."

Ṣaḥīh Muslim 1732

Hadith 25

قَالَ رَسُولُ اللهِ ﷺ

نِعْمَتَانِ مَغْبُونٌ فِيهِمَا
كَثِيرٌ مِنَ النَّاسِ
الصِّحَّةُ وَالْفَرَاغُ

niʿmatāni maghbūnun fīhimā
kathīrun minan-nās
aṣ-ṣiḥḥatu wal-farāgh

"There are two blessings
that many people are
deceived into losing:
health and free time."

Ṣaḥīh Bukhāri 6412

Hadith 26

قَالَ رَسُولُ اللهِ ﷺ

خَيْرُ النَّاسِ مَنْ طَالَ عُمُرُهُ
وَحَسُنَ عَمَلُهُ

khayrun-nāsi man
ṭāla ʿumuruhu
wa ḥasuna ʿamaluhu

"The best of people is the
one whose life is long,
and whose deeds
are excellent."

Sunan al-Tirmidhi 2329

Hadith 27

قَالَ رَسُولُ اللهِ ﷺ

يُبْعَثُ كُلُّ عَبْدٍ
عَلَى مَا مَاتَ عَلَيهِ

yubʿathu kullu ʿabdin
ʿalā mā māta ʿalayh

"Every person will be resurrected in the state upon which they died."

Ṣaḥīh Muslim 2878

Hadith 28

قَالَ رَسُولُ اللهِ ﷺ

تَهَادُوْا تَحَابُّوا

tahādū taḥābbū

"Give gifts to one another
and you will love one another."

Bukhāri in al-Adab al-Mufrad 594
Abū Ya'lā in al-Musnad 6148

Hadith 29

قَالَ رَسُولُ اللهِ ﷺ

أَتَاكُمْ أَهْلُ الْيَمَنِ
هُمْ أَرَقُّ أَفْئِدَةً وَأَلْيَنُ قُلُوبًا
الإِيمَانُ يَمَانٍ وَالْحِكْمَةُ يَمَانِيَةٌ

atākum ahlul yamani
hum araqqu af'idatan
wa alyanu qulūban
al-īmānu yamānin
wal ḥikmatu yamāniyyah

"The people of Yemen have come to you. They are more gentle and soft-hearted. Faith is from Yemen, and Wisdom is from Yemen."

Ṣaḥīh Bukhāri 4388

Hadith 30

قَالَ رَسُولُ اللهِ ﷺ

كُلُّ أَمْرٍ ذِي بَالٍ
لَا يُبْدَأُ فِيهِ بِالْحَمْدِ لِلَّهِ
فَهُوَ أَقْطَعُ

kullu amrin dhī bālin
lā yubda'u fīhi bil ḥamdi
lillāhi fahuwa aqṭa'

"Every matter of importance
that does not start with
the Praise of *Allāh*,
is devoid of blessings."

Sunan Ibn Mājah 1894

Hadith 31

قَالَ رَسُولُ اللهِ ﷺ

إِذَا مَرَرْتُمْ بِرِيَاضِ الْجَنَّةِ فَارْتَعُوا

قَالُوا: وَمَا رِيَاضُ الْجَنَّةِ

قَالَ: حِلَقُ الذِّكْرِ

idhā marartum bi riyādhil jannati farta'ū
qālū wa mā riyādhul jannah
qāla ḥilaq-u-dhikr

"'When you pass by the
gardens of Paradise, then graze.'"
The Companions asked:
'And what are the
gardens of Paradise?'
He said: 'The gatherings
of remembrance.'"

Sunan al-Tirmidhi 3510

Hadith 32

قَالَ رَسُولُ اللهِ ﷺ

الْمُسْتَشَارُ مُؤْتَمَنٌ

al-mustashāru muʾtaman

"The one who is consulted is entrusted."

Sunan Ibn Mājah 3745

Hadith 33

قَالَ رَسُولُ اللهِ ﷺ

لَاَ ضَرَرَ وَلَاَ ضِرَارَ

lā ḍarara walā ḍirār

"It is prohibited
to cause harm,
and it is prohibited
to reciprocate harm."

Sunan Ibn Mājah 2341

Hadith 34

قَالَ رَسُولُ اللهِ ﷺ

مَنْ خَرَجَ فِي طَلَبِ الْعِلْمِ
فَهُوَ فِي سَبِيلِ اللهِ حَتَّى يَرْجِعَ

man kharaja fī ṭalabil ʿilmi
fa huwa fī sabīlillāh ḥattā yarjiʿ

"Whoever goes out
seeking knowledge,
then they are striving in the
way of *Allāh* until they return."

Sunan al-Tirmidhi 2647

Hadith 35

قَالَ رَسُولُ اللهِ ﷺ

خَيْرُكُمْ خَيْرُكُمْ لِأَهْلِهِ
وَأَنَا خَيْرُكُمْ لِأَهْلِي

khayrukum khayrukum li ahlihī
wa anā khayrukum li ahlī

"The best amongst you
is the one who is best
to their family, and I
am the best of you
to my family."

Sunan Ibn Mājah 1977

Hadith 36

قَالَ رَسُولُ اللهِ ﷺ

مَنْ كَانَ يُؤْمِنُ بِاللهِ وَالْيَوْمِ الْآخِرِ
فَلْيَقُلْ خَيْرًا أَوْ لِيَصْمُتْ
وَمَنْ كَانَ يُؤْمِنُ بِاللهِ وَالْيَوْمِ الْآخِرِ
فَلْيُكْرِمْ جَارَهُ
وَمَنْ كَانَ يُؤْمِنُ بِاللهِ وَالْيَوْمِ الْآخِرِ
فَلْيُكْرِمْ ضَيْفَهُ

Hadith 36

man kāna yu'minu billāhi
wal yawmil ākhir
fal yaqul khayran aw liyaṣmut
wa man kāna yu'minu billāhi
wal yawmil ākhir
fal yukrim jārahu
wa man kāna yu'minu billāhi
wal yawmil ākhir
fal yukrim ḍayfahu

"Let the one who believes in
Allāh and the Last Day
speak good, or keep silent;
and let the one who believes in
Allāh and the Last Day
be generous to their neighbour;
and let the one who believes in
Allāh and the Last Day
be generous to their guest."

Ṣaḥīh Muslim 47

Hadith 37

قَالَ رَسُولُ اللهِ ﷺ

مَنْ حَفِظَ عَشْرَ آيَاتٍ
مِنْ أَوَّلِ سُورَةِ الْكَهْفِ
عُصِمَ مِنَ الدَّجَّالِ

man ḥafiẓa ʿashra āyātin
min awwali sūratil kahf
ʿuṣima min ad-dajjāl

"Whoever learns by heart
the first ten verses of
Sūrat al-Kahf will be
protected from the
False Messiah."

Ṣaḥīh Muslim 809

Hadith 38

قَالَ رَسُولُ اللهِ ﷺ

خَيْرُ يَوْمٍ طَلَعَتْ عَلَيْهِ الشَّمْسُ
يَوْمُ الْجُمُعَةِ فِيهِ خُلِقَ آدَمُ
وَفِيهِ أُدْخِلَ الْجَنَّةَ وَفِيهِ أُخْرِجَ مِنْهَا
وَلاَ تَقُومُ السَّاعَةُ إِلاَّ فِي يَوْمِ الْجُمُعَةِ

khayru yawmin ṭala'at 'alayhish shamsu yawmul jumu'ah fīhi khuliqa ādam wa fīhi udkhilal jannah wa fīhi ukhrija minhā wa lā taqūmus sā'atu illā fī yawmil jumu'ah

"The best day on which the sun has risen is Friday. On this day Adam was created. On it he was made to enter Paradise. On it he was expelled from it. And the Last Hour will take place on no day other than Friday."

Ṣaḥīḥ Muslim 854

Hadith 39

قَالَ رَسُولُ اللهِ ﷺ

إِنَّ مِنْ أَفْضَلِ أَيَّامِكُمْ يَوْمَ الْجُمُعَةِ
فَأَكْثِرُوا عَلَيَّ مِنَ الصَّلاَةِ فِيهِ
فَإِنَّ صَلاَتَكُمْ مَعْرُوضَةٌ عَلَيَّ

inna min afḍali ayyāmikum
yawmal jumuʿah fa akthirū
ʿalayya min as-ṣalāti fīhi
fa inna ṣalātakum
maʿrūḍatun ʿalayy

"The most excellent of your
days is Friday. So invoke many
prayers and salutations on me
on that day, for they will
be presented to me."

Sunan Abu Dāwūd 1531

Hadith 40

قَالَ رَسُولُ اللهِ ﷺ

مَا بَيْنَ بَيْتِي وَمِنْبَرِي
رَوْضَةٌ مِنْ رِيَاضِ الْجَنَّةِ
وَمِنْبَرِي عَلَى حَوْضِي

mā bayna baytī wa minbarī
rawḍatun min riyāḍil jannah
wa minbarī ʿalā ḥawḍī

"There is a garden of Paradise
between my house and my pulpit.
And my pulpit is on my basin."

Ṣaḥīh Bukhāri 1196

The Guiding Light

Illumination of brilliant radiance does not discriminate between objects it shines upon. Likewise, the light of Prophet *Muḥammad* ﷺ reaches all people, despite their faith or non-faith. Allah has stated his noble mission in the *Qur'ān*:

'And We have not sent you except as a mercy to all of creation.'
Qur'ān 21:107

In our current time, the world is in need of restoring relationships through mercy. We are in need of showing kindness to each other. We desire a world in which people can complete one another, rather than compete with each other. This is what the light of Prophet *Muḥammad* ﷺ offers us. A path by which our character, movements, and stillness can be illuminated.

Since the best amongst us are those who are best in character, a challenge remains before us: how are we to strive in making incremental improvements in our default nature and character traits? This becomes our lifelong quest. For some of the most important endeavours in our lives, we may resort to guides who are capable of showing us the way. These masters in their field raise a mirror to our face so we can observe our own, true, and confronting self.

Reflecting upon the life of the Prophet *Muḥammad* ﷺ grants us the honour of having an example of impeccable character to turn to, in every moment. We live in a short and transient existence. Our connection to this guiding light paves the way for a transition into the next phase of our human and soulful existence. A world far more dazzling in its radiance. Indeed, a worthy objective that outlasts temporary fulfilment of pleasures in this fleeting life.

And now, it is your turn. Whilst we can easily tune in to various radio frequencies and listen to a live transmission - your inner soul possesses a unique frequency. It emits countless signals with every inhale and exhale. Are you ready to listen to the inner voice of your soul, and seek to fulfil its innate desire for permanent contentment and lasting satisfaction?

'And my success is not but through Allāh.
Upon Him I have relied, and to Him I return.'
Qur'ān 11:88

www.ingramcontent.com/pod-product-compliance
Lightning Source LLC
Chambersburg PA
CBHW030418120726
47904CB00007B/2337